PATH TO HAPPINESS & PROSPERITY

APPLICATIONS FOR LIVING SERIES

PATH TO HAPPINESS & PROSPERITY

NEALE DONALD
WALSCH

JAICO PUBLISHING HOUSE

Mumbai Delhi Bangalore Kolkata
Hyderabad Chennai Ahmedabad Bhopal

Published by Jaico Publishing House
121 Mahatma Gandhi Road
Mumbai - 400 001
jaicopub@vsnl.com
www.jaicobooks.com

Published in arrangement with
Writers House LLC and
Hampton Roads Publishing Company, Inc.
Charlottesville, Virginia, USA

PATH TO HAPPINESS & PROSPERITY
ISBN 978-81-7992-680-2

First Jaico Impression: 2007

Printed by
Rashmi Graphics
Shop #3, Amrutwel CHS Ltd.
C.S. #50/74, Ganesh Galli
Lalbaug, Mumbai-400 012.
E-mail: tiwarijp@vsnl.net

Dedication

For
Dr. Leo Bush
and
Letha Bush

Who have given so freely to so many
of all that they are, and all that they have.

Through their lifetime of generosity
they have both demonstrated,
and received, their abundance,
serving as an inspiration and a model
for all who are blessed to know them.

Introduction

The greatest irony of life is that what all of us want, all of us have.

We have an abundance of that which we wish we had an abundance of.

You may not believe that this is true for you, or for others that you observe or know, but it is true, and it is only our thought about it *not* being true that makes it not *seem* true in our experience.

Perspective plays an extraordinary role in how we experience life. What one person calls "lack," another person calls "plenty." And so, our private definitions create our private experiences. And our definitions, or what I call our decisions about things, duplicate and enlarge themselves. What we say is so, is what will grow to be so.

How do I know? Because I'm a good listener. You see, I've been asking questions about abundance, abundant living, money, and this thing that some people call "right livelihood" for some time. A few years ago, I began receiving answers. I believe those responses to have come from God. At the time I received them, I was so impacted and so impressed that I decided to keep a written record of what I was being given. That record became the *Conversations with God* series of books, which have become best-sellers around the world.

It is not necessary for you to join me in my belief about the source of my replies in order to receive benefit from them. All that is necessary is to remain open to the possibility that there just might be something that most humans do not fully understand about abundance, the understanding of which could change everything.

That's the frame of mind that a small group of about forty people held when it gathered at a home just outside San Francisco, California, in January 1999 to explore with me more deeply what *Conversations with God* has to say on this subject. I shared with the group all that I understood about the material on abundance that appears in the dialogue, and answered questions as they came up. The synergy of that afternoon produced an electrifying experience, resulting in an open flow of wonderful wisdom that, I am happy to say, was captured on videotape and audiocassette—edited versions of which have since been made public.

This book is a transcript of that event, and reads in a much more free-flowing—and, I think, more stimulating—style than text that is written for the printed page. And because the book format is not limited by time and production constraints, we were able to include here material not found in the video or audio versions, which necessarily had to be shortened for production reasons.

Essentially, what God tells us in *CWG* is that most of us do not understand what abundance really is, confusing it with money. Yet when we take stock of that in which we truly are abundant, and choose to share it freely with everyone whose lives we touch, we find that what we *thought* was abundance—money—comes to us freely.

Even this chain of events, however, many of us cannot accept. For when we think of money, we imagine that it is an experience and an energy that stands outside of the reality of God. Yet there is nothing in the universe that stands outside of the reality of God; that is not a *part* of God. Once we understand that money is a part of what God *is*, our attitude about money changes. We see it as an extension of the glory of God, not the root of all evil. This can produce astonishing results.

It *is* possible to experience abundance, and the extraordinary insights in the *Conversations with God* books show us how.

Here are those insights, as I have received them and understood them. I share them with you here in humility, straight from the Take It for What It's Worth Department, with the hope that if even one comment opens a new window

or throws wide a doorway to greater happiness,
you will have been served.

Neale Donald Walsch
July 1999
Ashland, Oregon

Path to Happiness and Prosperity

Well, nice to see you all here. Good morning, everybody. Good morning, my darling. That's my wife. Good morning. I don't call everybody in the audience my darling. But I could be tempted to.

Well, I suppose you wonder why I called this meeting. And so do I. I'd like to start off our time together this morning just chatting a little bit about what happened to me in my life. I wanted to kind of roll into some of the experiences that I've had over the last six or eight years, bring you up to speed and up to date, and let you know what that was like for me. And we can go from there, and begin talking about some of the specific topics that I hope we have a chance to explore here together.

How nice of you to choose to be in the room with me on this day. And how nice of you to choose to be on the planet with me at this time. This is a very, very important time. People have said that for centuries, and they've always meant it. But I'm not sure it's always been quite as true as it is right now.

We're moving into a period of time on this planet when the decisions and choices we make will produce a critical impact and an extraordinary effect on the lives that we are collectively creating. So, it's really important that we come together in groups like this, groups large and small, and share our reality, share our understanding, become even more clear about what it is that we hold in common. And when we find that there are differences between us, find a way to celebrate those differences. Because if we don't learn how to celebrate our differences, we're not going to be able to *make* a difference on this planet. And you came here to make a difference. That's why you came to this body, at this time. That's why you came to this particular planet at this particular moment. Whether you know it or not, you came here with a very big agenda. And for most people, if you're like me, the agenda is much larger than you might originally have thought or imagined. I'm going to repeat that. I said: For most people, if you're like me, the agenda is much larger than you might originally have thought or imagined.

To begin with, your life has nothing to do with you. And that might change your whole idea about what you're doing here. And your life has nothing to do with your body. That also might change your whole idea about what you're doing here. Your life has to do with the agenda that has been set for you by you, by that part of you that we've come to call, in our language, your soul.

And it has been my observation that very few people have spent a lot of time during this particular life paying attention to the agenda of their soul. I know that I haven't. Most of my life, I paid attention to the agenda of my ego, of my mind, of my body—in other words, of that part of me that I thought that I really was. And I paid very little attention to the agenda of my soul, to the real reason that I'm here. And yet, those of us who begin to pay attention to the real reason that we're here begin to make an extraordinary impact on the world—an impact beyond anything that you might have imagined possible. Suddenly you find yourself at a . . . at a precipice, at the edge. And it is very much, as Apollinaire once put it, "Come to the edge."

"We can't. We're afraid."

"Come to the edge."

"We can't. We'll fall."

"Come to the edge." And they came. And he *pushed* them. And they flew.

There are a few of us, a very few of us, who are now ready to fly, who are ready to go, as Gene [Roddenberry] said, to places where no human has gone before—who are really ready to fly now, and to take all those whose lives they touch with them, on a flight of fancy that will truly change the world. And in these days and times, you will have an opportunity to decide whether you are one of those select few; selected, I might add, by yourself, not by anyone else. This is a self-selecting process. You'll wake up one day and look in the mirror, and say, "I select me. I choose me. I'm it." It's a game of tag, with only one player. "I'm it."

It is very much *like* a children's game, you know. It is very much like a children's game, played with the abandon and with the joy of children who play together—except in this game, there is only one player. And now you get to quit playing hide and seek, and you get to start playing tag. "I'm it." "You're it." "Thank you very much."

So, in these days and times, you get to choose yourself; or not, as you wish. As *you* wish. But if you choose yourself to play in this particular game, you'll find that you have caused yourself to set aside all of your prior beliefs, understandings, thoughts, and ideas about what it is that you are doing here, about why you brought yourself to your body at this time and in this place. You'll change everything you ever thought about that. And you'll find that your life, indeed, will have nothing to do with you, or with your body.

And yet the irony is that, in the moment that you decide and declare that your life has nothing to do with you or your body, everything you ever sought, hungered for, struggled to obtain for yourself and for your body will come to you, *automatically*. And you won't even care. Because you will no longer need it. You will enjoy it, for sure. But you will no longer need it. And the struggle will at last be over.

But it will have just begun for the hundreds and the thousands and, maybe, the millions of people whose lives you will touch. And you will see them every day—people for whom the struggle really has just begun, who are taking those first few steps on the journey home. And they, like you, will reach out a hand, figuratively, if not literally, and sometimes even quite literally. And they'll look around them, and hope to find someone who will reach a hand back, who will say, "Come, follow me"; who will *dare* to say, "I am the way, and the life. Follow me."

That may sound almost too religious for some people. But this is the third and the last of the children's games that the child in us, which is our soul, will play. No longer *hide and seek*; no longer *you're it*; now, *follow the leader.*

Follow the leader. And you're the leader. And we're going to follow you. We're going to walk in your footsteps. I'm going to make the choices that you are going to make. We're going to make the decisions that you are making. We're going to say the words that you say, touch the world in the way that you touch it. We're going to follow your lead.

If you thought that the whole world was watching you this day, and following your example in everything that you think, and say, and do, would it change in any way how this day went for you? Maybe for some of you, just a little bit.

Well, the whole world is following you, whether you know it or not. That's the great secret: the whole world—surely the world whose lives you touch—is following you. We're watching you. We're seeing who you really are. And we're seeing who you think that you are. And we're taking our cue from you. Like actors on a stage, we are imitating you, because we have no one else to imitate. We're all that there is. There's no one else.

We can look outside of ourselves for some larger example out in the sky someplace—maybe even in our imaginations. But in the end, we will imitate each other. In the end, children will imitate their parents, and parents will imitate their parents. And nation will imitate nation. In the end, we will take our cues from each other, until one of us steps out and says, "Not that way. This way."

So your decision at this time in your life, at this really critical period as we turn the century and move into what is truly a new age, your decision is critical. It's not a small decision. Because you're not making it just for you. The decision you make in these days and times, you're making for everyone else in the room. And the reason for that is very clear. Because there *is* no one else in the room. Except you. Here you are, in your many other manifest forms; here you are. And so the decision you make for you, you make for all of us. Because there's only one of us here.

That might sound a little esoteric. First we sound religious, then we sound esoteric. But it is these thoughts, these concepts, these ideas which must begin to drive the engine of our collective human experience, or our collective human experience will not be collective much longer, but will, in fact, disintegrate and fall apart, even as will our planet.

We are at that point now. You know when airplanes in the old days used to cross the ocean, they called it "the point of no return"? Too far to turn back, not far enough to safely make it there? There's this little red zone, you know, when you're neither there nor here, you're neither here nor there.

It feels very much as if that's where we are right now on this planet, in many ways: in terms of our ecology, in terms of our worldwide economy. We see, in many areas of the world, the whole thing is falling apart, in terms of our social structures, our spiritual understandings, the education of our offspring. In so many ways and in so many areas, it feels as if we're in that no-man's land, in that red zone. We're not here, and we're not there, either. Neither here nor there, but we're beyond the point of no return. We have crossed the Rubicon.

I'm giving away my age with all of these phrases. Anyone under thirty-five is saying: "'Cross the Rubicon?' What the hell is that?"

We've crossed the Rubicon, and now the question is: What do we do, and how do we get the rest of us to go over to the other side? And the answer to that question will be, in fact, supplied to the human race by people like you. By you.

And if you think it's about people like me who happen, in this particular day and time, to be enjoying our fifteen minutes in the sun, you're wrong. I want to impress on you here today that it's not about the people in the front of the room. I just happen to be here now by—I want to say—by sheer happenstance. It could just as easily be you. As a matter of fact, one of you just come on up here and do the rest of the program. (laughter) Just a thought. Nancy's ready.

But that is the real test. That is the real question. How many of you, if given the opportunity, if called to the challenge, if selected, would say: "Hey, Neale, you know what? I'm ready! I'll take the chair, I'll take the place in the front of the room." Because the real secret of life is that you're in the front of the room anyway, whether you know it or not. That's the point I've been trying to make. You're in the front of the room anyway. It just looks as if you're not. In fact, the real irony of life is that there's no place *other* than the front of the room. There's no back of the room. So, you can't hide out anymore. So, *follow the leader*, it turns out, is mandatory.

Let me tell you how I wound up in this chair, just to give you a little bit of background on how all this began. In 1992, I had reached the end of the line for me. In 1992, I had reached a point where I was losing again another committed relationship with a significant other. My career had reached a dead end. My health was falling apart. Nothing was working in my life. And this relationship that I had with my significant other was the one that I knew would last forever. And there it was, in front of my face, just disintegrating right in my hands.

It wasn't the first time that such a relationship had disintegrated right in front of me. Nor was it the second. Nor was it the third, or the fourth. And so (laughter) I knew that there was something I don't know here, that the knowing of which would change all of this for me—I just didn't know what that was. And in my relationship life, I simply couldn't find that secret.

And then in my career, I was having the same kind of challenges. You know, I had read all the books: *Do What You Love, and the*

Money Will Follow. I don't think so—unless it does, of course. But I couldn't seem to find the formula. I was either doing something that I did love, but I was dead broke; or I was making enough money to skim by, making it through, but my soul was dying a thousand deaths. I didn't seem to know how to put the two together. Not for very long. If I did get it together, it was always for about six or eight months, then it would all fall apart. I couldn't seem to glue the pieces together, and make them stick.

And likewise, my health: I couldn't seem to get through a year without something going on, and sometimes it was a pretty big thing that was going on. I mean, I had ulcers and I was thirty-six. I had lots of stuff happen: chronic heart problems, just a pile of stuff I'm not even telling you about. And so, at the age of fifty, I really felt as if I was eighty years old—and not a very healthy eighty years old at that: arthritis, fibromyalgia, just stuff going on. You know what I'm saying? I couldn't get this mechanism to work. All of this was happening at the same time.

Now, see, usually God had been better than that. It was usually one thing or the other in my life. But for this particular period, for reasons that still aren't clear to me, it was all at once, at the same time. "Oh," God said, "let's give him a triple whammy. Let's do the old career-relationship-body number in the same week." And so, there I was. It was kind of like a Triple Lutz, you know, kind of a metaphysical Triple Lutz. And I was skating on thin ice. I didn't know where to go with it. I was very, very, *very* angry—threatening to fall into chronic depression.

And one night I threw back the covers of the bed, because I had awakened in the middle of the night filled with rage and upset over how my life was. I stormed out into the larger part of the house, looking for answers in the middle of the night. I went to where I always go for answers in the middle of the night, but there was nothing decent in the refrigerator that night, so I went to the couch instead. And there I sat on the couch.

Try to picture that, sitting there in the middle of the night, four o'clock in the morning, on the couch, stewing in my own juice, as it were. Then I called out to God. I thought, well, I can run around and tear apart the house, break the dishes, or whatever. But I sat there and I called out, "God, what does it take? What does it take to make this game work? Somebody tell me the rules. I promise I'll play. Just give me the rules. And after you give them to me, don't change them." And I asked a ton of other questions as well.

And then I saw, on the coffee table in front of me, there happened to be a yellow legal pad lying there. There was a pen next to it. So I picked it up, flicked on a lamp, and I began to write my anger out, you know. Seemed to be a safe, quiet way to deal with it at 4:15 in the morning. I don't know how it is with you, when you are angry and when you're writing, but I write really big when I'm getting angry. And there I was. *What does it take?* I was really angry. *To make life work? And what have I done to deserve a life of such continuing struggle?* Exclamation point, exclamation point, exclamation point.

And on and on I went like that for about twenty minutes, just writing out my anger, you know, defying the universe to give me a response. And then I finally calmed myself down, just a bit, felt just a little bit better. And I felt okay. I thought, hey, that worked. I have to share this process with some friends. That works. I took the pen, and put it down, and the pen would not leave my hand. I looked at that, and I thought, "Isn't that interesting? My hand is cramped up from all that writing." You always find a reason.

I brought the pen back to the paper for reasons that aren't clear to me now. And a thought came to me. A little voice, right over here, just over my right shoulder. I call it now my voiceless voice. When I first heard the voiceless voice, it was very much as if someone was whispering in my right ear. And the feeling that came over me was one of extreme calm. I was, I want to say, becalmed—very much at peace and filled with kind of an indescribable joy.

You know, I think of moments in my life when I've had that joy . . . the moment that I married Nancy—not even the whole ceremony, but that particular moment when the minister finally said, you know, "do you . . . "And in that moment I looked in her eyes and I just paused for a moment and said, "I do." There was just that tiny sliver of a moment when your whole body is filled with something you can't describe, and you realize that you're making an enormously important decision, a huge choice, and that you're so glad about it that there's not even a tiny bit of doubt about it—that moment of total gladness . . . joy really.

I think all of us have had those moments, maybe three or four, perhaps five times in a lifetime, when we just are filled with that sense of "rightness" . . . this is totally right, this is totally joyful. That's how it felt in that moment when I first heard that voiceless voice. Just . . . joy. A peaceful, calming joy.

And the voiceless voice said, "Neale, do you really want answers to all of these questions, or are you just venting?" I said, "Well, you know, I am venting, but if you have answers, I'd sure as heck like to know what they are." And with that the answers came—in a flood. The answer to every question I ever asked came to me. And so fast that I felt I had to write them down, or I would forget them. You see, I never intended to write a book. I was simply writing this stuff down because I didn't want to forget all that was coming to me.

So I wrote it down in a flood, as fast as my hand could fly. And as I read what I was writing, it brought up, naturally, other questions for me. Because it was astonishing stuff that was coming off the pen. So, I started writing the questions that the answers brought up for me, and that brought more answers. And I wrote more questions, and that brought more answers. And before I knew it, I was involved in an on-paper dialogue with what I later came to know must be God.

That's the short story of how I happen to be here—and wound up sending that on-paper dialogue to a publisher. People ask me, "Why did you do that if you weren't intending to write a book?" Well, you might recall, in the dialogue, it said "this will one day become a book." And I thought, well, I'll just test God. I was actually testing Deity. Because when I wrote that out, "this will one day become a book," my first idea was, "Yeah, you and a hundred other people are going to send your middle-of-the-night mental meanderings to a publisher, who's going to jump on them immediately, and say, 'My God, of course, *we'll publish this right away.*'" And millions of people across the world are going to buy this thing.

Except that's, in fact, exactly what happened. And it was published. And millions of people have purchased it. It's been translated into twenty-seven languages around the world. It's really astonishing to see something you've written come out in Japanese, or Greek, or

Hebrew, and to realize that, in fact, you've touched the entire world.

A Digression

Why am I sitting here in the front of the room? I want to tell you why I've chosen to be in the front of this room. I'm very clear now that I was called on to be a messenger. I'm very clear now that, in fact, I've always been a messenger, and that there's no place I can allow myself to be *except* in the front of the room. Because I have a very important message to share with everyone whose life I touch. And here is the important message I've come to share: *All* of you are messengers, and there's no place else for you to be except in the front of the room. All of you have come to share a very important message with everyone whose life you touch. And here is the important message that you have come to share with them: All of them, each of them, is a messenger. And they have come here with a very important message to share. And there's no place else they can be except in the front of the room. And here is the important message they have come to share: Everyone is a messenger.

And it was a dark and stormy night, and a group of bandits was seated around the campfire. And one of the bandits happened to say, "Chief, tell us a story." And the chief said, "It was a dark and stormy night, and a group of bandits was seated around the campfire, when one of the bandits happened to say, 'Chief, tell us a story.' And the chief said, 'It was a dark and stormy night . . .'"

So, you see, it's circular. The eternal story of life is the same story. The glorious message I've come to share is the same message. The message is that you have come to share a message. And the message you've come to share is that they have to come to share a message, and here's the message all of us have come to share with each other: "Hello, *wake up*. Do you know who you really are? Hello. *Wake up*. Do you understand?"

Here's the message we've come to share: You and I are one. There's only one of us in the room. If you think we're separate, cut it out. We're not separate. There's only one of us in the room. And there's no difference between us. And if you think there's a difference between us, cut it out. Because there is no difference between us. And stop trying to create an artificial difference where there is none. And when you can't, then you and I are one, and there's only one of us in the room, and only one of us on the planet, and only one of us in all of creation. Everything that causes you pain and misery, travail and struggle, heartache and difficulty, will disappear. It will simply go away.

So stop thinking that you're over there, and I'm over here. There's no place where "you" end and "I" begin—such a simple, elegant message that changes everything. When will we get it? *When will we get it?* We'll get it when we send it. Did you hear that? We'll get the message when we *send* the message.

So, here we are together today. I walked into the room and I thought, "What in the devil am I doing here? See, if I'm not careful, it's liable to look as if I have something to say that you don't know. I've got to be real careful about that. And if we're not careful, it could look to *you* as if you have something to hear that you don't know; that you've never heard before. If we're not careful, we're liable to forget who we really are, and we're liable to play a game called "I know, and you don't." Except that I'm not willing to play that game, now or ever. I'm very clear that there's nothing I have to say that you don't already know. So, thanks for coming, and goodbye.

I've been trying to figure out some way to get out of the room since I walked in here. That'll work as good as any. All right, before we go any further, because we're going to talk here a little bit about one of our most important subjects, which is the subject of abundance and right livelihood . . . But before we do, somebody had their hand up. And I've been ignoring it for fifteen minutes.

When you described you heard the voice, the left part of your shoulder . . .

Actually, it was my right shoulder, but who's looking?

And subsequently, when writing, asking questions, writing books, getting a response, was there a particular feeling associated with that particular voice or that particular impulse to write, that authenticated it over, say, other times we hear a voice, or other times we're urged to write? Was there something, something else, a presence or a feeling or . . . Can you describe that for us, what that felt like?

It was a softness. It felt as if my whole body had just turned into Jell-O. I almost don't know how to describe that. It was just a releasing of every bit of anxiety or tension, or I want to say, "negativity," within me, as I sat on that couch. I can recall just—almost as if, without any act of volition on my part—I'm going to release my tension here. It just happened. I just suddenly . . . and then, from that softness sprang a . . . It's sort of difficult to discuss this. I go right back into it, almost immediately.

Almost feels like a peace descended?

It's a peace and a sense of incomprehensible joy, and oneness—a joy that almost brings tears. That kind of deep, deep joy. And from that first moment, I just sat there, and the tears began to flow. Before I wrote more than ten words, I can recall the experience of the ink blotching on the page. I was using one of those felt-tip pens—and the ink was running as my tears were flowing.

I've kind of gotten used to the experience now. So, I'm aware of what's going to happen. But I know what it feels like. Have any of you ever been present at the moment that a baby is being born? And held it in your hands for those first three or five minutes of its life? If you've ever had that experience, that's what it felt like. It felt that way, like when I held my child for the first few moments of its life, and looked in its face. And there was no other feeling I could have, except oneness, complete connectedness, love that knew no limitation of any kind, and no condition at all. Just a sense of . . . You can't even put it into words, that's how it felt—like holding your newborn child in your hands. That's how it felt. And I knew, in that moment, that I was, in fact, holding a newborn child in my hands. I knew that I had given birth to a new Me.

You know, I've never said that before. Just in answer to your question, that imagery comes up for me. You'll know when you're reborn. No one has to tell you when you've been born again. You will know it. And you'll come out of that moment never again feeling the same, ever—about yourself or anyone else.

All barriers between you and other people will drop away. All sense of separation will disappear. And then you'll become very dangerous.

Because you'll want to walk up to people and give them great big hugs. You know, you'll want to just go to people and say, "I love you so much," (laughter) and hope they don't have you arrested—especially if, God forbid, you should do it to another man . . . . Because society says you're not supposed to do that to another man. If you're a man, be careful . . . same-gender stuff. You know, we have all of these . . .

Excuse me, I cry at my own material. (laughter)

From the beginning of time, all we have ever wanted was to love and be loved. And from the beginning of time, all we've ever done is create moral restrictions, religious taboos, societal ethics, familial traditions, philosophical constructions, all manner of rules and regulations telling us who, when, where, what, and how we may love; and who, when, where, what, and how we may not. Unfortunately, the second list is longer than the first.

What are we doing? *What are we doing?* If I walk up to this guy, and I say, "The beauty of me sees the beauty of you," what is wrong with that? Or if I walk up to a stranger, and say, "I see who you are," how is that not okay?

I don't understand how we've decided to construct it here, people. But I've got to tell you this: If we don't change the construction, we will never have the truest experience of who we really are. So, it's time to rebuild, and re-create. It's time, in fact, to re-create ourselves anew—in the next grandest version of the greatest vision we ever held about who we are.

Boy, oh boy, oh boy, oh boy . . . Don't get me going. See, you put me in front of a room full of people like this, and I see new members of the army. What can I do to recruit them? How can I get them to play, you know? Did you ever have that feeling when you walked down to the playground? I used to walk over the hill to the playground in our neighborhood. We had a big playground about eight blocks from my house. And as I got closer, I'd get excited: "I wonder who's there. I wonder who's there." As I'd approach, I'd see some kids out there playing around. Some of them I'd recognize, some of them I didn't know, from some other part of the neighborhood. I can always remember thinking: "How can I get them to play with me?" Did you ever have that feeling when you approached the playground?

Then you'd get to the playground, and some kids would say: "Hey. Hi, Neale. I'll play with you." And other kids would go, "Oh, it's big mouth Walshie again." And you'd get rejected. Anybody here ever get rejected on the playground? None of you, huh? None of you are former playground rejectees? That's how it feels when I walk into a room like this. "Oh, boy, I wonder if they'll play with me. Wouldn't it be fun if they did?"

So, let's play around a little bit with this material. Let's take a look at some of the things that have been told to me in this extraordinary dialogue that I found myself engaged in. Let's talk about abundance.

Abundance is a topic in which I have had a great deal of interest through the years. And so have many people. And the first thing I came to understand about abundance was that, when I began to look at it deeply, and when I began to receive my information from a higher authority, I have been mis-defining what abundance really is. I thought that abundance was stuff, that it had to do with how much stuff I had.

I hate to be simplistic here. I hate to be really obvious with what I'm going to tell you, because I know you already know this. But for those of you who have forgotten that you know, I'd like to remind you of what I was reminded of in my dialogue: True abundance has nothing to do with anything that I am having, and everything to do with what I am being. And that when I share my abundance of beingness abundantly with all those whose lives I touch, everything I sought to have came to me automatically, without my even trying to have them.

All the stuff that I thought abundance was about: all the fine crystal, you know, and the wonderful antiques, and the beautiful clothes, and all that, just kind of fell into place without my struggling for it. So that I was seeking what I thought was abundance, and it was just stuff. And that which I already *had* a great abundance of, I was virtually ignoring.

I recall sitting in a room full of people, a little bit larger than this, not too many weeks ago, when I was facilitating a retreat in the beautiful mountains of Colorado, in Estes Park. And in that room, a person said to me, "I wish I could experience abundance." That was his issue. And he said: "You know, I don't make a great deal of money. I have barely enough to get by. I had to really squeeze pennies to get here." And so forth. And he said, "I've all my life wanted to experience the kind of abundance that I see you"—and he pointed to me in the front of the room—"experiencing." And I said, "Well, you know, if you really want to have the experience of abundance, why don't you spend your lunch hour giving abundantly of that which you have to give." And he looked at me, astonishingly enough, and he said, "I have nothing to give."

He really thought—he wasn't even making that up—he really thought he had nothing to give. And so I had to look at him and begin to say the obvious. "Do you have any love to give?"

"Oh," he said, and he wasn't even sure about that. But, I think, he had to concede the point that perhaps there was a morsel of love within him that he could give. He said, "Yeah, yeah, I suppose I have some love to give."

I said: "Do you have any compassion? Does compassion reside within you at any level?"

"Yeah, well, I suppose I have a little bit of compassion. People have called me a compassionate guy."

It was hard for him to say that, by the way. He was having a hard time saying the word "compassion" in the same sentence as the word "me." But he allowed as to how, perhaps, he had some of that to give as well.

So, did he have any humor?

He said, "Oh, yeah . . . I got enough jokes to last for a lifetime."

I said, "Terrific."

We made a list of the things that he had in abundance. But, of course, he didn't think that had anything to do with abundance as he was describing it. I said: "Okay, let's agree that we disagree on our definitions of what abundance is. But let's agree that you do have an abundance of *these things*." We could agree on that.

I said: "Great. Now, here's what I want you to do. Spend your lunch hour, and I want you to give of these things that you have acknowledged that you do have in abundance. Give of them in profusion. Give more than you ever gave before, to everyone whose life you touch for the next ninety minutes, while we're on our lunch break. That's my challenge to you." And he agreed to accept the challenge.

And so he went off on the lunch hour, which was just a few minutes from that time, and he began to outpour that of which he had abundantly, to everyone in this YMCA camp where we were doing this retreat . . . there was not just our group, but groups from other places that rented different lodges, so there were maybe 600 people at this place; 200 of them were in our retreat, and 400 from other places. So, there were lots of strangers who didn't know who this guy was, or what he was up to. So, he walked into the cafeteria. It was like a major confrontation for him. Because it was like, my group knows that I'm going to act crazy now, but the rest of these people don't know that I'm now going to act kind of nuts.

You see, when you give of yourself abundantly, half the world calls that crazy. They say you must have some something going on with you, something's wrong. People don't act that way. Which, of course, is the problem. People don't act that way. So, here he is, walking up to people in the cafeteria, and he is sharing, abundantly, of that which is abundantly his. He's sharing of his love, and his good cheer, and his humor. He was telling jokes all over the cafeteria. Some folks were laughing, "Ha ha ha ha, that's pretty funny." And other folks were laughing, "Ha ha . . . Who is this guy?" But everyone couldn't help but laugh a little. And even those who didn't think his joke was that funny couldn't help but grin a bit at this wonderful guy, this "Santa" who just showed up in the cafeteria all of a sudden.

He was going around saying wonderful things to people. One person, it just happened, was not in that good of a mood, and it was his opportunity to show some compassion. And he showed compassion by not telling any more of his bad jokes. That can be an act of compassion, I have learned. But then he sat down next to that person. He said: "I don't know you, but I'm from this other group that's doing a retreat in the other lodge. Everything okay?" Before he knew it, he had become involved in a conversation with God. And he got to express that part of himself.

This guy came back from the lunch hour, ninety minutes later, feeling so huge, feeling so big. And he said, "I can't tell you how I feel." I said, "Do you feel abundance now?" He said: "Yes, I do. I feel abundantly wealthy. With all these grand parts of me that I haven't really given myself permission to express. Hadn't given myself permission to do that."

But what was really funny, and here's the trick that the group played on him . . . while he was at lunch, somebody went to the room and got their hat, and everybody in the room put money in the hat. So, when he got back to the room, the guy had a lot of money in the hat. Because the room just wanted to prove to him, you know, what goes around, comes around, and all that. It was just this incredible in-the-moment experience of the truth. Did you ever have one of those in-the-moment experiences of the truth? You just go, "Bong!" Palm to forehead, "Duh." Because it's just so obvious, and so obviously expressed.

So, after he sat in his chair, and told everyone about this, they handed him this pile of money. And he just sat there . . . the tears start to flow. And he had a direct experience of what is eternally so: That which you give to another, you give to yourself. And you can give it in one form, and it will come back in another. But it cannot fail to come back to you, because there's only one of us in the room. And his life changed out of his new awareness of what abundance truly is.

Even people living in the streets can develop a consciousness of abundance. First, they can do so by causing others to have that which they would choose to experience themselves. For as little as you have, you will find someone who has even less.

I'm reminded of the story of a guy named Joe who actually lived in San Francisco on the streets. And as little as he had, he made it his job every day to find someone who had less than he had. If he managed to panhandle a couple of bucks on the street, he'd give two and a half times that to someone who had even less. And he was a very abundant guy; he was known as the king of the streets, in fact, because he was the source of abundance for everyone else on the street.

People on the streets can begin to experience abundance if they are willing to allow someone else's life that they are touching to experience abundance in that moment. That might seem easier said than done—I mean, I'm sitting here in the lap of luxury making that statement. And I don't want to sound shallow. And I don't want to sound gratuitous. But I lived on the street. I lived on the street for nearly a year of my life. And I remember what pulled me out of it.

So, the first thing I want to share with you about abundance is: Get clear what abundance is. And if and when you decide to give abundantly of the grandest part of who you are, with everyone whose life you touch, if you decide to do that, your life will change in ninety days. Maybe ninety minutes. Be careful. Because people will suddenly get who you are.

Let me explain to you the difference between lawyer A and lawyer B. See, here are two lawyers, and they both have an office on the same block, in the same city. They both graduated from the same college, and they both graduated at the top of their class. So, they have equal skill levels. It's not about location, because they're both on the same block, in the same city. Yet, one lawyer, lawyer A, is doing fabulously well. And lawyer B, just a few feet down the block, is not doing so well. What's that about? What's happening there? What causes one person to be the thing we call successful, and another person not, given everything else being equal? Just to set up the discussion.

So, it's not about, well, he was born into wealth; and he was born into this; or he had that advantage. What about the case of two people where all the other things are equal? What's happening there? Lawyer A is very clear. Plumber A is very clear. Doctor A is very clear. It's not about what he's doing. It has nothing to do with what he's doing.

So, be careful that you don't get caught up in a thought that your abundance (or what you might want to call your success in life) will come to you out of what you're doing. It will not. And if you haven't learned that, life will teach you that. Because you'll do all this stuff. You'll be doing this, and doing that, and doing this, and doing that, and doing this, and doing that—and just wind up with a great big pile of do-do. And you'll wonder: "How did I create this pile of do-do here? I did all the right things."

And then it will dawn on you: "Oh, I get it. It has nothing to do with what I'm doing. That isn't the connection. That is not how all this good stuff that I think is going to flow to me, is going to flow to me." And then we see another person down the street who appears to be doing nothing. And abundance is flowing down upon them. Just can't push it away fast enough. That's not fair.

"How does he get to have all that? He's not doing anything." Which is, of course, precisely the secret. He's not doing a damned thing. I mean to say, and I chose my words very carefully there, he's not doing a damned thing. And we've been spending our lives running around doing all these damned things. But he's *being* something. When he walks into the room, he's being something extraordinary. He is being love, compassion, wisdom, humor, sensuality. He's being joy. And he's being One. The highest level of being is: He's being One.

You know, when you go to a doctor, lawyer, plumber, dentist, whoever it is, anybody to whom you're going, the clerk at the post office—doesn't matter—when you're going to that person, you look into their eyes, and you say: "They get me. They see me. They're . . . " in a sense, though you might not articulate it this way, "they're like one with me." We walk away, "What a nice person. What a nice guy. Wasn't she, wasn't she sweet . . . ?"

I always try to get in his line. You know what I'm talking about? You ever have that? When I go to the supermarket, I try to get in this one particular lady's line. Because she—I just get a hit off of her. And there's nothing going on—there's just something that—I want to be in that person's line. Because I go through that line, and I just get that hit, that special something that happens.

I finally wrote a letter to the postmaster. I don't know what that guy in the first line has got going for him, but there's a magic going on with him. He makes everybody in that lobby just magnetized and gravitate to where he is.

I asked this guy at the post office whether he feels abundant. I know he feels abundant. And it has nothing to do with his salary. Do you understand? So, that's what makes the difference. That's the difference between lawyer A and lawyer B, plumber A and plumber B. Person A and person B out there on the sidewalk. So, you get to decide whether you choose to be B person, or whether you choose to be A person. If you choose to be A person, person A, and give abundantly of all the magic that lies within you, the magic that lies outside of you will be attracted to you, and become as much a part of you as you allow it to become. Got it? We'll talk more about how that works in just a bit.

So, the important thing for us to remember, when we're searching for right livelihood, is to stop looking for something to do, and start looking for something to be. And to get in touch with that part that resides deep inside of you that knows who you really are. And see what it would take to call that forth in a *beingness* way.

So, look inside. What is it that I'm being, when I feel totally fulfilled and totally self-expressed? What am I being when that happens? Maybe I'm being a healer, maybe I'm being sensual, maybe I'm being creative. Or there's some level or state of beingness that would describe to you in a word or two the essence of what's showing up for you, what part of you that's really showing up big. And that's how we find our right doingness. It's when doingness flows from beingness, rather than us using doingness to *get* to beingness.

I'll explain all of this later, but before I get into it, as I said a minute ago, before I get into a detailed explanation of that, I want to go to some other thoughts, first of all, that I have noticed block people from experiencing abundance. And that have blocked me from experiencing abundance. And I am going to talk about abundance in terms of dollars and cents and physical things. Because it's okay, by the way, to call that abundance, too.

See, I don't want to make it sound as if I'm saying that that's not abundance, and that the only abundance there is, is the stuff we talked about before. It's also okay for us to call this stuff, this physical stuff (the money, and the cash, and the accouterments, the wonderful glassware and the antiques, and the beautiful physical stuff of life) . . . that's abundance as well. So, we don't want to eliminate that from the category of life experience that we call abundance. And that's another thing that I was doing. I mean, in a sense . . . I called it abundance, all right, but I didn't like it. Let me explain, if I can.

Many people hold the thought that money, per se, is bad. I don't know whether you hold that. And some people hold that thought almost unconsciously. That is to say, if you asked them directly: "Do you experience that money is bad? Is it your thought that money is bad?" they would say, "No, money is good." Many people would say that. But they act as if it's bad.

I'll give you an example. I knew a person who would never admit that she held the idea that money is bad. To her, in fact, money is good. But when she does you a favor, like drive you to the airport, two hours back and forth to Phoenix or something, and you get down to Phoenix, and say, "Let me give you just a couple of dollars for gas," you get: "Oh, no, no, no. I couldn't. I couldn't."

Did you ever have anybody do you a favor, and when you want to offer them a few pennies, just to kind of compensate for some of the hard costs they put into it, they won't take the money? What do you suppose that's about? They're happy to take your thanks. They don't want to take your money. Because somehow the exchange of money for the good thing they did for you, at some level, besmirches the exchange. You see, it drops it to a level that starts to feel icky.

By the way, that level would never feel icky to me. So, if anybody wants to give me money for doing something nice, just let me know. I'll take all the money in the room. That's hard to say sometimes, because people want to think, "Oh, Neale's a really spiritual guy. He shouldn't be saying stuff like that." But I am going to say that stuff.

There's a guy I once knew named Reverend Ike, who used to say, "I *love* money, and money loves *me*." And that's a great message: I love money, and money loves me. And I don't declare that, in my universe, God is everything except money. Rather, I declare God that is everything, *including money*; that money is just another form of the energy that we call God.

I don't know whether you've been reading the news lately, but just the other day, there was a huge story in one of the national newspapers about Red China. They're now having this incredible shift of consciousness there, where they're now telling the people about the virtues and the glory of earning and having money. Can you imagine that? This, in Red China, which, by the way, is one of the twenty-seven nations that have translated the *Conversations with God* books. We found out a few months ago that they've been purchased for translation by the People's Republic of China, of all places.

You see, the world is changing overnight in every one of its places. So, if the people, the peasants in Red China, are now starting to become clear about the glory and, I want to say, to "coin" a phrase, the okayness of money, and having it, don't you think we should? So, we need to get off of our idea that somehow money is bad.

You know, we talk about filthy lucre, and we talk about being filthy rich. We use phrases that give away what our inner thought is, or at least the inner thought of society at large, about this. And I can tell you that society still holds this thought very deeply. One of the questions I am most frequently asked by people at large, and by lecture audiences, and so forth, and by the media inevitably, when I get interviewed by one of the major media people: "How does it feel for you to be going around the country talking about spirituality, and making so much money at it?" As if somehow I'm doing something wrong, you see. As if somehow that should be a warning to the public . . . big warning. "See, look . . . look at how much money he's making off this."

And every so often I get a letter from somebody who says: "If you're really so spiritual, why don't you give away all of your royalties to the poor? Why don't you, for that matter, just put the book on the Internet, and let people have access to it for free?" And the reason that we don't do that is that if we did that, the publishers would go out of business, and the book could never be produced to begin with.

See, somebody has to do the first thing, called "publish the book" in some form. Even putting something up on the Internet costs money. I know, because I know some people who put things up on the Internet, and they want a lot of money for it. So, because that's true, what we notice is that money is just the lubrication that makes the machinery of life work at this present time on our planet, as society is currently constructed. And that's all right. See?

So, I refuse to go to that place that says if you were really a spiritual person, you'd give your book away. You'd take the royalties that you do get for it, and spread it out among the poor. And you wouldn't take any of that for yourself. As it happens, just as a matter of information, Nancy and I and the foundation we have created do contribute a large sum of money each year to many many worthwhile causes. That's not important. It's just what's true. It's just what's so.

But, you know, I love making a lot of money. Because it allows me to do a lot of things, and I'm very clear what I want to do in the world. I'm very clear the changes that I want to cause to happen. And as I said, in our society, it takes that lubrication to make that occur.

I think we have to forget everything we've ever learned about money. I really think we have to erase the blackboard and wipe the slate completely clean. Even those of us who have been blessed to have a bit of money in their lives sometimes have a hard time dealing with that—and being okay with it. Because virtually every message we've received about money makes money the bad guy, the villain, and, by extension, those who have it become the villains in life, even though people are not villains, even those who have a great deal of money. We've got this mind-set about money. Money is the root of all evil. We call it filthy lucre and people who have a lot of it are said to be filthy rich. There's something dirty about it—something unclean. And it's almost as if those who do have a little bit of it maybe got it some way that was undeserving, that it wasn't fair or it's not okay for them to have it. So there's this huge myth about money . . . I call it the money myth. And the money myth in human societies is that it's really not okay, which is interesting, because everyone wants it. So that puts everyone in a position of wanting something that it's very not okay to have.

It's a little bit like sex. It's the same way. I don't know very many people who don't want as much sex, good sex, at least, as they can get. But it's very not okay in most places in our society—see I'm not really joking about this—I'm being quite serious—it's very not okay in our society to want a lot of sex. And if you just come out and say, "I want a lot of sex," people think that somehow you're deranged or you're not okay in some way. Money is the same way—even more so.

You know if you walk down the street and ask people about their sex lives, they'll actually talk to you about that. But ask them how much they have in their bank account. Watch their face go crazy. "You want to know *what*? What I have in my bank account? I beg your pardon, that's very personal." Who you slept with last night is not [personal]—well a little bit—but this is *really* personal. You're talking about money here. So people have even more of an emotional charge about money than they do about their own sexuality. Interesting, isn't it? It has to do with all of the messages we've received all of our lives about money—nine-tenths of which have been very, very, negative.

So, how to become friends with money? First, you have to forget everything you've ever been told about it. And then you have to put in its place a new message: There's nothing in the universe that isn't God. And God, and the energy which is God, is found in everything, including money. It isn't like God is everywhere except in your billfold. In fact, God *is* everywhere.

We need to understand that money is simply another form of the energy of life, and a very, very powerful form, not powerful in and of itself, but powerful because we've given it power. We, as a society on this planet, have said, "We grant this particular medium of exchange enormous power in our lives." And that should really render it totally okay. We've given it our blessing. We've said that we value this more than that. We value gold, for instance, more than dirt, unless it's dirt in some particular place that can turn into gold very quickly—called real estate. But we have blessed something, and then condemned it, at the same time, you see; it's an interesting contradiction. Again, just as we've done with sex. We bless the act of human love that demonstrates itself in a sexual response at the same time we condemn it. It's extraordinary. All of that behavior springs from an even larger cultural myth. And the larger cultural myth that many religions have given us, I'm sorry to say, is: "You're not to enjoy yourself." And since sex and money are two ways that we can enjoy ourselves, we've made them both wrong—terribly, terribly wrong—and created enormous dysfunction on the planet, and in our own personal lives.

How to make friends with money? Imagine that money was a gift to you from the universe with which to do every good for yourself and for others that you ever wanted to do. Now we have yet another hurdle to get across. "Oh my, if I have a lot of money, I can actually do good things for myself. I could actually go out and buy a very expensive suit, or $550 Italian shoes." Do I dare even say that I'm wearing $550 Italian shoes? Actually I am. Do you know how long it took me to be okay with a pair of $550 Italian shoes? I mean, this is not about the shoe; it's about what this represents in my life. And it doesn't represent that I have the money to afford it. It represents that I have the mind-set to make it okay for me to have this. Do you understand that that's a huge graduation?

I want to share what's made it possible for me to make this graduation. Because this is about more than this sole . . . this is about *this* soul—and the soul in each of us—so that *everyone* can walk, ultimately, in these shoes. Figuratively and literally, everyone can walk in the same shoes . . . when they learn this lesson: There is no part of life whatsoever that is not a part of God. There's no aspect of the life energy whatsoever that is not holy and sacred. Nothing is evil, lest thinking make it so. Let us stop making money evil. Let's stop making sex evil, and most of all, let's stop making each other evil.

What are we doing here? And why are we doing it? Why do we insist on seeing evil and negativity in every corner of our lives? What is that about? That's the question. That's the larger question. That's the central question. And as human beings, we are at a focal point now. We are at a critical juncture—we've come to cusp with the largest question, that really has nothing to do with money, but with life itself.

Do we see life and all of its elements as essentially evil, or as essentially good? That's the question. If we see life as essentially good, we'll solve our problems with money and we'll make money our friend. And then we'll do good things with that money, good things for ourselves because we deserve it. I deserve these shoes. And so do you. And then we'll do good things for others. We'll share the abundance that is ours, and the abundance that is given to us by God, with all those whose lives we touch. And no one will be without anything. There's enough for all of us. And when we choose that, we'll be friends with money, with ourselves, with everyone else, and with God.

So, what we have to do is to get comfortable with money, as we have to also get comfortable, I might add, with our bodies, and with each other. We have to learn to get comfortable with the stuff of life, so that we can say, "Bring all that life is to me, and all that I am a part of, life, I bring to you," and not be ashamed of any part of it. Because God doesn't know from shame.

So, here's your chance to just drop your ideas about money not being okay, about money being somehow bad. This is what causes people to stay in lives of quiet desperation. Because, since they think that money is bad, and don't like to take any bad thing for a good deed, they wind up doing a job they hate, that at least they can justify getting money for. So, they spend eight hours a day doing a job they hate, then they do something they love as a volunteer. They go to the hospital, or be the leader of their Boy Scout troop, or whatever they're doing. So, they do what they love for nothing, and they do what they hate because they can accept money for that. Because, after all, who would do that for free? Who would do that for free?

But everything changes when you make a decision to be one of the courageous ones, someone who chooses to make a life, rather than a living. And that's when your whole experience shifts. You create a shift beyond belief when you change your thought about what you're up to here; when you decide, in fact, to make a life rather than a living. And that shift is so enormous that everything is altered in your experience, including your experience of money. And make no mistake about it, this is possible. I'm here to tell you that shift happens. Now, we have a question over here . . .

So, a conflict I have with money . . . I also appreciate it, enjoy it, and I used to feel like I would have to do things I didn't want to do to get money. Now I see that's not a problem. But the conflict still left for me is that I feel like, if I have a lot of money, I'm participating in a program or system that leaves the majority of the world on the outs. That would be much more acceptable for me if I knew that everyone in the world had food, everyone in the world had medical care, everyone in the world had housing and clothing. And then money was simply a means to play with more (quote-unquote) unnecessary . . .

I hear every word you're saying. But be careful that you don't use your righteousness about that to deprive yourself of the very empowering instrument that could cause it to happen *through you*. Be very careful that you don't use righteousness to *disempower yourself* from being one of those who can actually *cause that to happen*.

My life is dedicated to creating a world exactly as the one you just described. But I can tell you that I'm far more effective in doing that now, than I was when I was denying the very power that would cause me to be able to create those kinds of changes.

One of the biggest traps of the human experience is righteousness. And sometimes we feel we have, I want to call it, "a right to be righteous." I mean, we really feel that we have a firm grasp on right and wrong in any particular situation. And, within the framework of that relative system of thought, we might, in fact be dead right about something. It's a very dangerous place to be, though. Because righteousness can block effective action more quickly than just about any other kind of attitude or experience. It stops us from being understanding, you see.

When I think I'm right about something, I can't begin to understand how you could hold a point of view different from me, or how a condition can be allowed to continue. I lose my compassion for the people who created what I'm being righteous about. When I lose my compassion, I lose my ability to make any kind of really effective change for the better. Because no one likes to be made wrong.

It's especially dangerous, I think, for us to become righteous about all the wrong that's being done in the world. Because being terribly righteous about what's wrong in the world is a huge announcement that we don't understand that we've placed it there.

Let me give you an example: How would it serve a great surgeon, or a great doctor, a great physician, to be righteous about all the illness and sickness in the world? How would it serve a wonderful barrister, an extraordinary attorney, to be righteous about all the conflict in the world? I mean, he may want to change the conflict and reduce it, but to be righteous about it, to make it wrong that there is so much conflict, would fly in the face of what he himself is creating in his own reality, in order to experience himself as who he really is.

You see, what we do as human beings is, we set the pins up, then we knock them down. What we do as human beings is, we create the exact, right, and perfect set of circumstances (I'm speaking metaphysically now) to allow us to express a part of ourselves that announces and declares who we really are. If who I really am, for instance, is a healer, I will create, metaphysically, the perfect set of circumstances to allow myself to express "he who heals." I will, therefore, bring into my experience, and even, at some level, *create* in my outer reality, illness. The opposite of that which I am, that I might express and experience who I am.

The worst thing that could happen to the world's ministers would be for everyone to reform tomorrow. They'd have nothing to say to anyone. So ministers, men and women of the cloth, will spend the rest of their lives, at some deep metaphysical level, creating that which needs to be spiritually healed, in order that they might express and experience who they are. That's why real masters judge not and neither condemn. They go about changing the outer circumstance of their world without condemning it. Because to condemn it is to condemn the very process by which they have been allowed to express a part of themselves that announces and declares the glory of who they are. This is a deep metaphysical mystery, but masters understand it perfectly.

Again, I repeat, that's why masters *never* condemn or judge anything, but simply seek to express a part of themselves that allows the exterior circumstances to shift and to change. On a practical matter, just from a standpoint of practical politics and practical social interaction, righteousness never serves anyone.

One of the most extraordinary public figures of our time, in my personal opinion, is Jimmy Carter. He's a man who moved into very explosive political situations without righteousness. And as a result of that, he changed many of those circumstances for the better, in ways that people who move into those circumstances with righteousness could never do.

> *And my righteousness or anger as to how the world is, in a lot of ways, is a major obstruction . . .*

No question. Every moment of righteousness and every moment of judgment stops you from expressing the grandest idea. Because no one can hear you anyway. When you speak from righteousness or judgment, no one can hear you. But not only do you push away the *power* that would cause you to be able to create, you push away the people that could even *bestow* on you that power. Because no one gets righteousness, *not even those you are trying to help.*

You also said something else interesting. You said that, in the earlier days and times when you contemplated these issues, you would catch yourself doing something you didn't want to do, or thought you had to do things you didn't want to do, in order not to "sell out." Yet no one does anything they don't want to do. Let's get very clear on this. No one does anything they don't want to do—ever. We just do what we want to do, given the results we anticipate it will produce. Then we pretend there was no other way, and convince ourselves to feel bad about the choices we've made. See?

No one does anything they don't want to do. No one. Can anyone in the room think of a time when you did anything at all that you didn't want to do? Can anybody . . . Who would raise their hand now? But, I mean, seriously, is there anyone in the room . . . Raise your hand if you think that there was a time in your life when you did something you did not want to do. Okay, let's go over here . . . .

I don't think it's that we don't want to do something. But what I hear around me, and I've learned not to do that from the books, is people saying, "I don't have any other choice." I think that people think that they don't have any choice, because I know that I've been there for a long time. And I used to say, "I don't have a choice." Because I didn't see, at that point in my life, another choice. But when I read the material, and I understood, as you say, we don't do anything without making a choice, I now make a conscious choice to do and to choose to do, and I even say out-loud to myself, "I choose to do that." Now, first, I choose and then I do. And when I hear, you know, "I don't have a choice," I always want to go in and say, "You know, you made that choice." But I think that in our society, it's really not acceptable. It's like having money. It's like I can't make my choices. It's too good. I don't know if I deserve that . . . I mean, there are more I-don't-have-any-choice people than I-choose-to-do-so [people]. Because it took a lot for me to change that.

There is never a time in life when you do not have a choice, ever. As a matter of fact, you have created the circumstances of your life, including this place that you call "no choice," precisely to give you an experience of the choices that you have. You've actually created this apparent roadblock to cause you to notice that there was no roadblock to begin with. And some of you will notice that. And most people will not. And they will allow themselves to live the rest of their lives imagining that they have no choice.

"I had no choice" is the most frequently used rationale for us doing what we wanted to do. We go ahead and do what we want to do in order to either *avoid* a particular outcome or *create* a particular outcome, which is really one and the same thing.

So we do what we want to do, given the circumstances that are in front of us, to either avoid or create an outcome. And then we say, "I had no choice." But you *do* have a choice. And every choice you make, every decision you make, every thought you think, every word you utter, is an announcement and a declaration of who you think you are, and who you choose to be. Every act is an act of self-definition. And you always have a choice. But remember this: No one ever does anything inappropriate, given their model of the world.

So, not only are you always given a choice, you are always making a choice, and you're always making the choice that you think will best produce, or avoid, a given outcome. What you seek is the outcome that will assist you in defining Who You Really Are. That's what you are up to. Now, you may not articulate it in that way, but I assure you, that's what the human soul is up to. And when you begin to see it that way, when you begin to frame it in that way, you see life in a whole different way. And you imagine life to be a grand adventure, because suddenly it becomes an extraordinary adventure—an adventure in self-creation.

Some people feel victimized about money. They don't really get, they don't really understand, that they're always at choice in their lives about anything, and especially about money. It seems to some people that they are at the whim and whimsy of the winds of fortune, to use perhaps a well-chosen phrase. Or the winds of misfortune, as the case may be. And they see, really, no connection between their monetary situation in life and their consciousness . . . the level of their consciousness. They don't make a connection with what's happening with them financially and how they're creating it . . . yet, I'm telling you that we create everything in our lives.

And so some people say, "You don't understand, Neale, you know I haven't had the opportunities other people have had." They've been disadvantaged, or they don't have the skills, or whatever it is that they imagine stands between themselves and money. I would say to them a number of things: first, money doesn't come to you because of what you do. If you think that money comes to you because of what you do, then, of course, you'll have all of those doingness alibis: "I didn't get my college education," or "I was disadvantaged to begin with," or "I haven't had the opportunities you've had"—because you're going to imagine that money flows to you because of something you're doing, rather than something you're being.

Beingness is something that everyone has, regardless of their education, their station in life, their ethnic or cultural background, their social status. Everyone can be loving; everyone can be extraordinary; everyone can be generous and giving and compassionate and friendly. Everyone can be all the things that we pay people big money to be, regardless of what they're doing. See, it doesn't really matter. The lawyers that make the most money, the doctors that make the most money, the ministers that make the most money, the paperboys that make the most money, are the paperboys that show up with an enormous smile on their face, a huge open heart to everyone whose life they touch. They're the ones that go around and get huge tips from the people they're delivering papers to, and all the other paperboys are wondering how they did that. "Oh, see, you've got a better bike," or "you have a better family background," or "you have a better neighborhood" or "you've got a better route."

No one in life has a better route. All we have to do is share with each other a level of beingness that others recognize as something they want to be touched by, all the time. And if we're willing to do that, it doesn't matter what our doingness in life is. We can be plumbers, paperboys, street cleaners, or corporate presidents. But all the good that comes from life will come to us in life when we are willing to open our heart and share, from a deep level of beingness, the treasure that resides within us, which is called love, or, loosely, friendliness. You know, a smile will buy you more goodwill than you could ever imagine.

So I want to say to people who think that they're the victims of their own monetary situations, look at those who have made it in life.

And take any cross section of people who have become very, very wealthy—any hundred millionaires—and you'll see an extraordinary cross section. Yes, you'll see some people who had all the advantages, all the cultural and social opportunities, and you'll see many who have not. And look at those who did not have any more than you have now, and ask them how they got from where they were to where you want to be. What is the difference between the two of you? And if they have the articulative skills, they'll tell you the difference: "I was willing to show up, *ta dah*! I was willing to give everything I had inside of me. It didn't matter to me."

Talk to Barbra Streisand some time. Just chat with her some time. Ask her about cultural and ethnic background and disadvantages and advantages. Then ask her how she got to this place. Some people call it *chutzpah*. Some people call it magic. Some people call it a certain *joie de vivre*. But what it comes down to, ultimately, is a willingness to just *show up in the space* as the wonderful "you" that you are, regardless of your story. You do that, and you'll be happy in life. By the way, you'll be happy in life *whether or not you have a lot of money.*

Neale, I wonder if you could tell us why so many spiritual seekers or so-called light workers seem to be up against it financially? Those of us who left our corporate jobs and are sort of called to do our right livelihood. And yet the testing ground seems to be: Can you make it through the financial fire? Why is it that so many of us have that going on?

Because the moment you declare yourself to be anything, everything unlike it will come into the space. I'll say that again: The moment you declare yourself to be anything, everything unlike it will come into the space. And it has to. It's the law of the universe.

"Why?" you ask. Because that's the way the universe works. And here is why:

In the absence of that which you are not, that which you are, is not.

Did you get that? You're shaking your head, my dear, and saying, "What is this guy trying to tell me?" I said, "In the absence of that which you are not, that which you are, is not." Now, let me give you an example. Are you big, and tall, and fat? No. How do you know that you are not big, and tall, and fat?

Compared to other people, I seem to be somewhat medium.

So, if big, and tall, and fat didn't exist, how would you know that you were not big and tall and fat? Supposing that everyone looked like you. God, wouldn't that be great? Oh, actually, you all look great just the way you are. Just a little one-liner that I can't resist. But what is your name?

Karen.

Karen. Supposing, just for the sake of this discussion, that everyone looked exactly like you. How would you know how you looked?

How would you know how to describe yourself? How would you be able to say: "I'm the one with the long, dark . . . Oh, I see *everyone* has long, dark hair. Okay, I'm the one that's relatively slim, and I'm kind of short. Well, actually, *everyone* is short and kind of . . . " How would you be able to even know who you were? You wouldn't, would you? Not in this relative existence.

Not on the outside.

No, not on the outside. And if everyone were identical on the inside, you wouldn't even know the inside of you. Because you'd all be the same. No? Therefore, I promise you that if you want to have a direct experience of who you are, and what you are, you will attract to yourself, like a magnet, everything that you are not. Because in the absence of that which you are not, that which you are, is not. Got it? Bingo.

Now the secret, the secret, once you know this, is to not resist it. Because what you resist persists. And what you look at, disappears. What you hold, and embrace, you make your own. What you make your own, no longer resists you.

Neale, there are so many people on this planet who are terrified to leave their corporate jobs, for fear that they'll lose their livelihood—all the security they've ever known. What would you say to them?

Some people *are* terrified to leave their corporate jobs. They're trapped in a prison of their own devise, because they have this idea that if they leave that corporate setting, or that position that they've worked so hard to attain, then all will be lost. And yet all is lost now, because if it wasn't lost, they wouldn't want to leave. So the key question is not, what will you lose should you remove yourself from that position, but what will you gain? And what even causes you to stop and think about leaving? That's the key question.

When you look at why would they even think about leaving, there must be something not okay with where they are right now. What's missing? It's about filling in the blanks.

And so what I would say to people who are in that place of dilemma, is what I've often said to people: You know, you need to make a life rather than a living. You might be much happier making one-third of your income, but coming from a place of beingness that brings joy to your soul.

See, that's the key question for everyone: When do we get to bring joy to our soul? Now, if what you're doing to make a living is bringing joy to your soul, how wonderful for you. But I have to tell you that that is a very small minority of people on this planet. Most people are living lives of quiet desperation, doing what they think they *have* to do in order to survive.

My life has taught me that we don't have to do anything in order to survive. I've always thrown caution to the winds, and I've always done what brought my soul the greatest joy.

That has made some of my friends and associates, my family members, and so forth, call me irresponsible from time to time. But to whom do I owe this great sense of responsibility anyway, if not to myself?

So I have refused to be unhappy for very long in any kind of occupation or activity that I was undertaking simply because I thought I had to, in order to maintain a standard of living. And I would do that again today if what I was doing now wasn't making me very happy. Even if I allowed myself to imagine that the happiness of others was my responsibility, how can I begin to make others happy if I'm desperately unhappy in my attempts to do so?

So, what I would say to people who feel trapped is, take a little test. Write down on paper: "traps I am in." And then describe the trap that you're in. "I'm in a job that I really don't enjoy, but if I leave it I won't be able to earn the money that I'm earning, and I won't be able to have all the things that I'm having for myself and the people who depend on me." Okay?

That's a trap. Then, "What would happen if I got out of this trap?" And then, after you look at what would happen if you got out of this trap, look at the third level. "What would happen if I did it anyway?" You see? What you'll find out is that the world will keep on spinning without you.

I learned a great lesson from an extraordinary woman many years ago. Her name was Dr. Elisabeth Kübler-Ross, and I came to know her personally. And one day Elisabeth and I were driving down the road together, and I said that I really wanted to do something, but it would require me to quit my job in order to do it, and I didn't think that I could do that for a lot of reasons, not the least of which was there were many other people depending on me to be where I was.

Elisabeth looked at me quite calmly, and, in her heavy Swiss accent, said to me, blinking very slowly, "I see, and vhat vould all dees people do, do you sink, if you simply died tomorrow?"

I said, "Well, that's an unfair question, because I'm probably not going to die tomorrow."

And she looked at me, and she said, "No, you're dying right now."

In that moment I decided to live. I decided to live my life. And that was the greatest decision I ever made. And that's what I would say to anyone who feels trapped, whether in a corporate job, or in any place in life. How much of your life are you willing to give away? And how much of your life are you willing to reclaim? And, once you reclaim your life, how much more do you think you'll have to give to others? Not just of material things, but of the joy and happiness that now reside in your soul.

That's why masters never resist the opposite of who they are, but, rather, see it as the grandest blessing. Bring on the opposite, bring on that which I am not. For I will not only welcome that which I am not, I will merge and become so much a part of it, that it will bless that which I am, and cause it to have grand expression. See?

All the universe is a field—a field. Some people call it a morphic field. I call it a field of experience, a field of expression. Life expressing *life itself.* It's a contrasting field, a field of contrasting elements, if you please. And it is only within this field of contrasting elements that any particular element can know and define itself as what it really is. That's true in the relative universe.

Now, in what I have been told is called, in our language, the Realm of the Absolute, such a contrasting field is not necessary—nor is it, for that matter, even possible. Because the Realm of the Absolute is, by definition, absolutely what it is. Do you understand? And there is nothing else. And we call that God. In my language, in my utterances, in my form of expression, we call that God.

In the beginning there was All That Is, and All That Is was all there was. And there was nothing else. There was nothing else except All That Is. And it was very good. But it's All That Was. And there was nothing else.

And yet, It sought to know Itself in Its own experience. And so It looked outside of Itself for something other than what It was, that It might know Itself in Its own experience. But It could find nothing outside of Itself other than what It was. Because there was nothing outside of Itself. And there was nothing other than what It was. Because It was All There Is, and there was nothing else.

How then, to know Itself in Its utter magnificence? And so that which we call God sought to look outside of Itself, but there was no place outside of Itself to look. It therefore looked within, that It might know Itself—not, incidentally, such a bad idea, should *you* choose to know yourself. Look within, and not without. For those who fail to go within, go without.

And so God looked within, and in the interior of that which is God, did God see all the magnificence for which It searched. And It literally imploded. That is to say, God turned Herself inside-out for us, and imploded into a thousand, cozillion, cajillion different parts—going here and there, up and down, left and right. And all of a sudden, here and there, up and down, left and right *were created.* Fast and slow, big and small were suddenly *created* in that glorious moment in that first thought that produced God in Its cajillion elements, each one of the elements racing from the center, at a thing that was now called Speed, and created the illusion that we now call Time. Each of the elements could look back at all the rest of God and say, "Oh, my God, how wondrous Thou art."

And all the other elements of God could likewise look back at the individual element, making that observation, and say to that individual element the exact, same thing. Only the individual element has not heard It. The individual element of that which is God has failed to hear the collective of that which is God say to It, "Oh, my God, how wondrous Thou art." And so, that which is the Collective called God leaves it up to the individual elements of God to remind each other: "Do you see how wondrous you are? Oh, my God, how wondrous Thou art."

And when we fail to say that to each other, when we fail to bring each other that message, we fail in the grandest mission of all. For we have come here to know ourselves. We've come here to know ourselves. Yet, I can only know me through you, ultimately, because there's only one of us in the room.

But, should you declare yourself to be abundance personified, that which attracts all the grand abundance of the universe, including money, I assure you that one of the first things that will happen is, you'll have the direct experience of having no money at all. Anybody ever had that experience? The moment you say, "Abundance is Mine, sayeth the Lord," as opposed to "vengeance" . . . there's a new bumper sticker huh? "Abundance is Mine, sayeth the Lord." Wouldn't that be interesting? The moment you say that, it will appear in your universe as if it's all gone away. And you'll start traveling, by the way, in circles where no one has any money, until you don't anymore, until you meet someone who is fabulously wealthy. And then, everything will change.

> *What about tithing, contributing 10 percent of income, and what of companies giving 10 percent of their net profits? Could we not shift the economy of this land?*

Conversations with God makes a rather extraordinary statement. It says that the day will come on this planet when we will move into a voluntary expression of sharing. And in that voluntary expression, everyone will take 10 percent of their income, voluntarily, and contribute it. Corporations will, individuals will, contribute it to a general fund, which will then be redistributed to people who are in need, and to social programs that serve those in need. On the day that we do that, all taxes will disappear from the Earth, because we'll raise more money by simply asking people to voluntarily give 10 percent than we could ever raise with taxes.

And no one will ever feel impinged upon, and everyone will give 10 percent of their income, high or low, whether they earn a thousand dollars a week, or a thousand dollars an hour, or a thousand dollars a year. You'll simply give 10 percent to the General Fund. And there will be an income level beneath which we won't ask people to do that; if you're only earning a dollar a year, we're not going to ask you to give us the dime.

But the construction, the economic construction, is based on a simple thought: that when you return a portion of what is coming to you to that Whole System, you, of course, enhance and enrich the System itself, and then more can come to you. The obviousness, if I can coin a word . . . that's not really a word I guess . . . but the obviousness of that is so clear, it's remarkable that we haven't caught on. But there's something even more important that happens when we tithe, whether we tithe to a church, to a synagogue, to our place of worship, or tithe to charities, or in some other way regularly set aside a portion, generally 10 percent, of what we have as income, for someone else.

When we tithe that way as a regular thing, we make an enormous statement to the universe. And that statement is, *there's more where this came from*. There is so much of this that I can literally give away, on a planned basis, 10 percent of it, and not even miss it. And that statement that we make in the universe is a statement of sufficiency, of "enoughness"—and in fact, it produces that in our experience. That's why so many spiritual movements say, tithe, tithe, *tithe*, not because we want to get your money, not even because we need your money, but because *you* need to make that *statement of sufficiency*. And it becomes a cellular command to yourself and to the universe. You really command the universe to produce the response that such actions would necessarily generate. So, tithing becomes a tool with which we instruct the universe about what is true for us.

This leads right into my next question: What lies ahead for the U.S. economy? What can you foresee in the twenty-first century? What might change? And what about the barter system?

You know, I really don't have a personal vision for the twenty-first century. What I know is that tomorrow will be created by the lot of us. My mission is to affect people right here, today, here and now.

If I had to look at the twenty-first century in response to your question, I would say that my grandest vision for the twenty-first century is that first of all, all of us come from two principles—economically, spiritually, politically, socially. We would come from two principles. The first principle is that we are all one. Do you imagine what the invocation of a principle such as that, we are all one, would do to us economically on this planet . . . and politically and spiritually? It would produce such upheaval and such shifting and such change that we almost can't describe it. And it would be all change for the good, for the better, of course. Wars would end, tomorrow. Disagreements would be virtually impossible; certainly disagreements that lead to violence would be very difficult to sustain, given the thought that we are all one.

And I envision, that sometime in the next century, and hopefully sooner rather than later, we will construct an economic reality around that basic spiritual truth: There's only one of us. And it is possible to do that. That economic reality would eliminate all thoughts of ownership. *Conversations with God* does go into this a bit, and it talks about a future in which no one will really own anything, but merely be allowed to act as stewards for certain things. You know, in the old days we actually thought we owned not only things, but people. I mean, husbands thought they owned their wives, and husbands and wives thought they owned their children, and it was like that. And so it was very easy to go from there to thinking they owned the plantation or the farm, or whatever.

But in the future it will be just as obvious to us that we do not own the earth, any more than we own our children. We've now finally grown to the place where we're clear we don't own each other. Husbands don't own wives; wives don't own husbands. By the way, that's only dawned on us in the past fifty years—it's not like it's been around for a long time. In the past thirty years, probably, we've gotten clear at last. That's a new thought for most of us cave men. And we've gone from that thought to finally releasing our sense of ownership over our children, and realizing we don't own them any more than we own our spouses.

And now we're getting to a new thought: We don't even own the land beneath us, just because we have a deed to it, much less the sky above us. Some people think like governments and say, "This is our sky . . . how high up is up?"

You know, we had a huge confrontation in the U.N. long ago because satellites were flying over the territorial space of a particular country, leading to an extraordinary question being debated in the U.N.: How high up is up? How much above a certain land area do you own? To the end of the universe, or where? We began to see how ridiculous we were being about it. Then how far down is down, of course? The minerals beneath your ground—are they yours? Does Saudi Arabia, with no offense meant toward any particular place on the earth, actually own the resources beneath the earth, the oil? And if they do, how far down is down? Some would probably argue, to the end of the earth—coming out on the other side.

That means that everybody owns everything, by the way, because if you really own the earth beneath you as far down as you can go, that means you own the earth on the other side of the earth. So, I don't want to make the question ridiculous, or the answer either, but the point is that sooner or later we'll evolve to a level where we understand we don't own anything, and we're simply stewards of it. And, when we get to that place, we'll stop despoiling the land, destroying the environment, and doing the kinds of things we're doing to Gaia, to this planet, because we think we have a right to, because, after all, it's ours. "This property is mine. I get to do with it what I want."

I envision an economy in the twenty-first century where the kind of ownership that allows us to destroy something at will, because we bought it, ignoring completely the effects that it has on the rest of us, will no longer be possible.

And then I see a second level to the twenty-first-century economy. I see a place where finally we are clear that there's enough—that there is enough of what we think we need to be happy for us to finally share it.

You know, there's enough right now on the planet; but there are millions of people who would argue with you. They would say: "You know, Neale, you can sit there and talk about sufficiency and enoughness, but we're starving out here. We don't have enough food. We don't have enough shelter. We don't have enough clothing. We don't have enough money. We don't have enough of the good things that you apparently have in abundance in your life."

Well, it's true, they don't have enough, but not because there isn't enough of the stuff around, but rather, because those who have it are not willing to share it. It's no secret that nine-tenths of the world's resources are being held in the hands of one-tenth of the world's people. Is that fair? Is that okay? Is that appropriate in a society that likes to declare itself and describe itself as elevated, as aware, as highly evolved?

By what manner or means, by what level of reasoning, can a society of evolved beings allow themselves to justify one-tenth of the people holding nine-tenths of the resources? Refusing to share them equitably by saying, "You don't understand, it's mine, I bought it, I worked for it, and you can't have it." It's remarkable that the nine-tenths of the world's people who are not allowed easy access to these resources are not revolting more than they are every day and creating more havoc than you could ever even imagine.

It's remarkable, and the only reason they are not in larger numbers is because of the goodness of the human heart, and also, because of the ignorance in which most of the world's people live. That's why there is a great hesitancy on the part of the establishment to allow the world's less fortunate to be educated. You see, knowledge is power, and the more that people know, the more they begin to see how extraordinarily unfair our system of economic distribution, and our distribution of resources, is on this planet.

So I envision an economy in the twenty-first century that looks at the obviousness of all of that, and begins to see the unfairness of it as well, and finally, at last, does something about it. And you know what's interesting about all of this, if I can conclude? We *can* do something about it, without necessarily taking away so much from those who currently hold the nine-tenths of the resources that they feel deprived. I can't even begin to tell you how much could be taken from me before I feel deprived.

I lived on the street. I spent nearly a year on the street, picking up cans in the park, living on the five-cent deposit. I've been there. I know the difference between that and where I am right now. And you could take nine-tenths of what I now own and take it away from me, and I still wouldn't be at that level, or even close to it. How much is enough? That's the question that is placed before the one-tenth of the world's people who are holding nine-tenths of the resources. How much is enough? And how much do people have to suffer in order for you to feel that you've got enough? And that, by the way, is not an economic question. *It's a spiritual one.*

To follow up on her question with regard to abundance. In the first book, the notion of manifestation, I guess you would say, proceeds from thought to word to ac-

tion. And there was a suggestion there that if one wants to begin to manifest, we need to reverse that process. To act "as if." And I wonder if you'd care to comment on that, as a piggyback to this other conversation.

Yes, while there are three levels—thank you. There are three levels of creation. So, we are each of us three-part beings, made up of body, mind, and spirit—just as God is made up of body, mind, and spirit. So each of us is an individual duplication of the triad of energies that we call God. And that triad, in our language, I call body, mind, and spirit. And so we each have three centers of creation, or three tools of creation: body, mind, and spirit.

What you think, produces energy in the universe, and if you think it often enough and long enough, it will actually produce a physical result in your life. Anyone experience that? Sure, most of us have. In fact, a guy back in 1946 wrote a huge, best-selling book on this called *The Power of Positive Thinking.* That new-age writer was Dr. Norman Vincent Peale.

Our second level of creation is words. As you speak, so will it be done. And so, your word is really a form of energy. You're actually producing energy in the room with what you say. And that energy is creative. If you say something often enough, loudly enough, I promise you it will come to pass. If two or more start saying the same thing, I assure you it will come to pass. And when a whole group of people starts saying the same thing, it cannot help but come to pass. This is called group consciousness, and it's, by the way, why the world is the way it is. Because our collective consciousness has not allowed itself to be raised to the level of the individual consciousness of many of us. So, our job is to raise the collective consciousness.

There is nothing more powerful in the world than collective consciousness. Every teacher from every spiritual tradition on the planet has said, in one form or another, "wherever two or more or gathered." And it is true.

The world that we see, and everything that we see in it, was once a thought. And most of the things we see resulted from the thoughts shared by more than one person—by many people. That is entirely true of most of our institutions, our political and educational and spiritual and social constructions, our economic constructions as well. So, if we can shift and change collective consciousness, we can shift and change the paradigm of our entire experience on this planet. That's why everyone is trying to do that. That's what mass media is about. That's what politics is about: shifting and trying to re-create group consciousness.

We now need to see a shift in *how we are trying to shift* the collective consciousness. We've had enough of politics already, and enough social impact on group consciousness. How about some spiritual impact on collective consciousness? If we can create a new collective consciousness of our own spiritual truth, the highest truth that resides within the deepest place inside all of us, we will change the world literally overnight. Overnight!

That's why books like *Conversations with God* are so important to this planet, and such a threat to certain places within the establishment. Because they create a direct pipeline to collective, or group, consciousness.

Is group consciousness important? You bet it is. That's why we have to be very careful what we allow on our television screens and in our movie houses, and in the books that we buy. We need to be careful what we're exposing our minds to, and what we choose to expose the minds of others to.

The effort should be to create and to re-create, really, a new collective consciousness, and an awareness of the collective. By that I mean, a collective awareness of our collective experience. In truth, what I'm saying is, what is needed now is a universal awareness of our oneness—the fact that there really is a single collective, and that we all belong to it. And nobody is outside of that. And nobody within that collective is better than anyone else. What an extraordinary idea.

Now, our actions, of course, are the third level of creation—that which we do with this huge, huge collection of energy called our body. This is a very gross level of creation—very gross level. I mean, I'm moving the air right now. Just moving your hand through the air is a huge, huge movement of energy here. You can literally push energy toward someone.

Anyone ever come up to you when you weren't feeling well, and just stand there with their hand on your head, and do nothing else? And in five minutes, you can begin feeling that—five seconds, sometimes—feeling that warmth, that vibration. And doggone it, sometimes, if you don't say, "I don't know what you just did there, but do I feel good."

Now, of course, if you go even further than that . . . I'll do this here with this lady who happens to be my wife. If you go even further than that, and actually touch each other, incredibly magical things can happen. It's the energy . . . .

Incredibly magical things can happen. Because the energy is very gross and not very big. Very heavy, very, very real.

Now, the problem we have in life is that, most often, people think one thing, say a second thing, and do a third. They do not, as the kids would put it, "have it all together." So they think one thing and they do another. Or, they say one thing, and they think another. Or they don't say what they're thinking, or they don't do what they're saying. Now, I know that none of you in this room have ever had that happen to you in your life. But, in my experience, there have been times when I have encountered that conflict between the three centers of my creation. So, I often do not want to tell people what I'm actually thinking, because I'm not real proud of what I'm thinking. Then why are you thinking it? God only knows.

Or, sometimes, lately, I've started to monitor my thoughts. And when I get a thought in there that I no longer choose, that's not really who I am, I don't give it a second thought. I literally don't give it a second thought. I just throw it out. And if you don't give it a second thought, it no longer has power. It's the nice part about this energy, that it's very thin, very ethereal. And you have to keep thinking it, and thinking it, and thinking it, and thinking it over and over again, until it's thunk so much that it becomes very heavy with collective energy. That's why Pogo said (Walt Kelly wrote that wonderful comic strip, "Pogo"), "We have met the enemy, and they is us."

So, life begins to change for you when you begin to say what you're thinking and do what you're saying. And then you have it all together. And you start to create from all three centers of creation. And suddenly, you begin to manifest and produce extraordinary results in your life in a very short period of time.

What was the question?

In regards to the message I got from reading that section, in terms of moving from thought, word, action. And the suggestion was that if we reverse that, then that can affect the manifestation that we wanted. And I wanted to have you elaborate and go into more detail about that . . .

Thank you. Thank you for getting me back on track. Got to be careful with me, because I'll just talk right out of the topic. Actually, I've stayed on the subject, almost. So thought is the most ethereal form, or, I want to say, the thinnest—to use a simple word—the thinnest form of this creative energy. And then your word is the next thickest—to use a simple word—the next most dense. And then, of course, your action, I started to say, is a real dense form of moving energy around. So, one of the fastest ways to create something in your physical reality is to reverse the normal process by which we create things.

Usually we create things first by thinking about them. "I think I'll go to that party." And then we say something about it. As in: "Matilda, I'm coming to your party tonight." And then we do something about it, as in showing up at the party. "Here I am. Just as I said I would be." Because I thunk the thought this morning. That's generally how we produce things in our reality.

In fact, everything in this room was once a thought in someone's mind. There is nothing that was not once a thought in someone's mind. But, if you really want to play tricks with the universe, and create magic with the stuff of life itself, reverse the thought, word, deed paradigm. Turn it upside down, and start with the deed. That is to say: act as if.

Now, we've been talking about abundance here during this time we've been sharing. If you want to experience abundance, *be* abundant, and do as abundance does. Therefore, if you have only five dollars left to your name, go to a store and get them transferred, made into singles. Take five singles, and walk down the street, and give a single to each of five people who have even less than you do. And by the way, you will find those people very easily. You will always find, in your experience, someone who has less than you, no matter how little you think you have. Not because the world is such a terrible place, but because *you will create it in your reality* in order to give yourself the experience that I'm talking about.

So, you'll walk down the street. And you'll see . . . now, by the way, when you see this person who has less, don't feel sorry for them. "Get" that you put them there. You created that experience. You put that person in your reality. And this is kind of like you've got to believe in fairy tales, like *Touched by an Angel.* You've got to notice that this is how it happens. Otherwise you'll see that little soul, and you'll start to have pity on that soul. Do not come from pity with anyone. Come from caring, come from love. But get clear: love is not pity. As a matter of fact, pity is about as far from love as you can get. So do not come from pity, but come from compassion.

Compassion says, in your mind, "Oh, there's a person who thinks they don't have what they could have in life. There's a person who still is caught in a belief system that creates a construction around their reality that's other than my own, and other than the Ultimate Truth." And have that compassion, but never have pity.

But also be clear that that person may just have shown up there by prior arrangement. I think I'll play a wino on the street today. In fact, I'll rehearse my role for thirty-six years, so that at 4:45 this afternoon, as Neale Donald Walsch is walking down the street, he can meet me here by prearrangement, and I can show up this way in his life, to give him an opportunity to notice that he is abundant. And he is going give me that dollar, one of the last five he has, and it's going to shift my reality of life so much. Because, to me, a dollar is an enormous amount of money. I'm getting nickels and dimes from folks on the street out here. This guy's giving me a dollar. And then I'll walk on my way, having fulfilled my contract for thirty-seven years to show up that way on that street corner.

Get very clear, nothing happens by accident. We cross each other's paths in the most mysterious ways, and find each other again, twenty years later sometimes. And there are more things in heaven and earth . . . undreamed of in your philosophy. So, be clear. There are no accidents, and there are no coincidences.

And so you walk down the street, and you give the last of your five dollars away. Now, what happens there? What's going on? You've reversed the thought, word, deed paradigm. You're now doing what the person who comes from abundance would do, and you begin giving away what, an hour before you made that decision, you couldn't imagine giving away, because you thought you didn't have enough. But now you are clear that you have more than enough—so much more, that you choose to give it to others.

Now, as you're giving this away, you're creating in your body, which is a very gross level of energy, an experience. The body is noticing cellularly: "Oh, my gosh, I'm giving this money away. Look at this. I'm even letting it go." It's kind of like in church on Sunday mornings. You know what your thought about your money is. When the basket comes around in church on Sunday morning, and you start pulling out those dollar bills. "I'm giving a whole dollar. Did you see this, Mildred? The basket there. Wow, a great sermon this morning. I'll make it five. Big sermon."

Pull out a twenty. Bring your checkbook out, and write a *hundred.* Let your church know how important it is to you. If you go to church, or go to synagogue, or go to a place of worship, and it serves you, pull out your checkbook and write a check for $150. Do it just once. Let your church, your synagogue, your place of worship, know. "This is how important this place is to me. I spend this kind of money on all kinds of nonsense, much less *sense.* I spend this money on nonsense." And do that wherever you see something that makes sense to you. Give, give, give, of whatever you have, to that which makes sense to you. And you will discover that it makes sense *for* you. *Dollars and sense.*

For that which you give to another, you give to yourself, because what goes around comes around. Money loses its value the moment you try to hang onto it. Money only has value when you're willing to let it go. Get that, for those of you who are saving your money, you're not *saving anything.* You know that it's even true in the world economy? The longer you save money, the less it's worth. To make up for it, we have to have some artificial construction called interest rates in order to convince you that holding on to money allows you to increase its value. You're lucky if the longer you hold onto money, you manage to maintain its value.

No, no, no. Money has its greatest value when it *leaves your hand.* Because it empowers you to be, do, and have something that you choose to be, do, and have. *Money's only value is when it leaves your hand.* But we will create these artificial, as I said, these artificial economic constructions called interest rates, and so forth, to convince you to horde your money. Save a little if you want to. It's all right. I don't save very much myself. I just kind of keep it moving, keep it moving. You know, just keep it going out there.

But the answer to your question is that, when you change the Be-Do-Have Paradigm, you start *acting as if*, and your body begins to understand, at a cellular level, who you think you really are. When I was a kid, my father used to say, "Who do you think you are, anyway?" I spent the rest of my life trying to answer that question. And my body is trying to understand what I think about that.

As my body starts moving into a field of gross energy, it starts moving things around—begins to give things away, for instance. All of a sudden, my body . . . Well, like your hair—you train your hair, huh? I train my hair. I've combed my hair this way now for years. My hair is trained. Your whole body can be trained, not just your hair. Your whole body can be trained like that. And your body starts getting the message: "I have that which I would choose to receive. I already have it." Now, once you cross that huge barrier . . . everything changes. Because you think you don't have it, and you're trying to get that which you do not have, namely more money. But once you get that, you *have* it; then it just becomes a question of how many zeroes are after the first number. Do you understand? And so, you'll discover that what goes around, does, indeed, come around. Not because you performed some real true magic trick of the universe, but because you finally got the truth of who you are. At some universal cosmic level. The universe never says no to your thought about yourself. It only grows it. Did you hear what I just said? I said the universe never says no to your thought about yourself. It only grows it. The universe is really wonderful. Because God grows on you. See, God is like the manure of the universe. I thought I would say something absolutely outrageous. Completely outrageous. Total juxtaposition, to see whether your minds can hold the most outrageous thought. Because—and I meant that in the kindest way—because God is that which makes things grow, makes things grow. And it will make you grow. Does that help a bit?

So whatever it is you think you'd like to be, do, or have, here's the secret, here's the truth: whatever it is you think you would like to be, do, or have, cause *another* to be, do, or have that. See yourself as the *source*, rather than the *recipient*, of what it is you would choose to experience in life. For you are not, in fact, the recipient, but you have been, and always will be, the source. When you imagine yourself to be the source of that which you wish you could receive, you become very *resourceful*. And then, you do become a magician. You do become a magician. You might even be called a "source-er-er."

You still have a question? I'm going to be as clear with you as I possibly can be. What is your question?

I hear that, and I understand it, and I get that. I wondered if you could address the issue that there is a resistance within one's self, that one encounters in doing, because there's still the belief, the fear, that if I give it away, then I won't have it. So, it's the resistance that is the rub, so to speak. And I'm curious to know how you deal with that.

If you want to know what you truly believe, if you want to really get in touch with the belief systems that are, I almost want to say running your life, look at what you're resisting. And most importantly, look at what you're resisting changing.

There's no mystery there; we resist what we don't want to let go of, and what we don't want to let go of is what we truly believe. So, this isn't a mysterious construction; it's stating the obvious. And yet, sometimes it's the most obvious thing that we ignore, and don't really take a look at. So I always tell people when I see them mightily resisting any suggestion, any change, any idea, any concept, look to see if that might be a very deeply held truth within you . . . that which you are resisting changing. And then look to see whether holding on to that truth as you are, with such white knuckles, is really serving you. Really take a close look at whether that truth serves you. It's amazing how few of our deeply held truths actually serve us. It's remarkable.

And when I took a kind of survey of the truths that I was holding deeply inside of me, and measured them against the question, "Is it serving me to hold on to this truth?" I surprised myself with the number of deeply held truths that I chose to then let go of, right then and there. I've had some remarkable truths in my life, including simplistic ones that are almost embarrassing to announce, like, "I'm not really a very attractive person." I mean physically very attractive.

Let me tell you something about that. I want to share something with you. This has nothing to do with money. But I want to just share this with you. I can recall once, I was with a very, very attractive woman. Beautiful woman. And I was standing in front of a mirror—we were getting ready to go out for the evening; we were sharing home space together. And I looked at her in the mirror and I said, "You know, you're so gorgeous, why would you want to be with a person who looks like me?"

Isn't that an interesting thing to say? Shows you what a low level of self-esteem I had. But I said it anyway, and she shocked me with her response. She was brushing her hair. She threw the brush down on the vanity, took off the earrings that she was just putting on, and threw them down on the countertop, began to take off her necklace—and I said, "What are you doing?"

She said, "I'm not going out with a person who thinks so little . . . " and I thought she was going to say, "of himself." She said, "Who thinks so little of me."

I said, "What? Who thinks so little of you?"

She said, "Do you think I have such horrible taste; is that your thought about me? I want you to know that I have very good taste, and you're insulting me when you ask a question like that."

I never thought about it that way. It's interesting, isn't it? I'm not even sure why I told that story, except that it made it very clear to me that I didn't understand. I had a strange idea about myself that she didn't hold at all.

So, I made this list of these beliefs that I had been resisting changing, everything from the simplistic belief about my not being an attractive person, to *much more* important beliefs: God is not on my side; the world's a tough place to be; everyone is against me; you can't beat the system; to the winner go the spoils; survival of the fittest—very deeply ingrained truths that had been running my life. And it's remarkable, the number of those truths that do not serve me.

So I say to people when I see them resisting something: Take a look at that. That's where your truth lies. Then look to see if that truth serves you. I'm willing to wager, eight times out of ten, that that truth no longer serves you. Did it serve you at one time? Possibly. Does it serve you now? I don't think so. Yet what you resist, persists. And only what you look at, and own, can disappear. You make it disappear by simply changing your mind about it.

I just feel the resistance and ignore it. Simply because now I know better. Because what I know is: What you resist persists, and what you look at, disappears. So, whenever I feel resistance to anything, I know that that is where truth lies, just beyond that resistance. Whatever resistance appears anywhere in my reality, I know that just beyond that is where the grandest truth resides. And because I know, I welcome that feeling, you know, that feeling of discomfort. See, life begins at the end of your comfort zone.

Now when I say that life begins at the end of your comfort zone, what I mean is that it is on the other side of your comfort that your challenge will be found . . . your greatest opportunity will be found. The tendency of all of us is to stay comfortable. Not just physically comfortable, but in fact, more often, mentally comfortable. When we're mentally comfortable, we're mentally stagnant as well. We're just, kind of like, blobbing out there, mentally, and spiritually as well. And the excitement in life is at the edge of all of that. It's on the other side of where we are comfortable. The danger of being comfortable, of course, is that we don't grow. We learn nothing, and we do not expand at all. We're comfortable all right, but we have really produced nothing in terms of expansion or growth in the largest part of our life.

So, I always look to see what is making me uncomfortable, and I move into that. Because it is what is making me uncomfortable that will ultimately make me larger, and cause me to grow and become a bigger version of myself, a bigger version of who I am. Therefore, in my life, anything that makes me uncomfortable, I take a closer look at.

I'll give you one more example: I was watching a movie about eight or ten years ago—it was a foreign film, not American—and there was a very vivid love scene on the screen. It was a very dynamic love scene. There was lots of nudity and lots of specificity in this love scene. And I was getting very uncomfortable about that. I was watching this thing and I thought, "Now, what about this is making me uncomfortable? How come I can watch Sylvester Stallone blow the heads off of people right in front of my face and I don't have any discomfort at all about it? Incredible violence, that I just watch and I'm a bit bemused by it, but I'm not terribly uncomfortable. And yet, here I am watching this scene of sexual love, this scene of passion fulfilled, and there's a part of me that's a bit uncomfortable."

That was about eight or ten years ago, and I looked at that for a long time. What about that was making me uncomfortable? I moved into the question, and found some answers that completely changed my whole life, and my whole experience of myself around sexuality, around other people, around my willingness to celebrate an aspect of myself that's so much a part of my basic nature.

I also changed my mind about violence. Now I watch violence on the screen and I have the precise, same reaction that I used to have when I watched overt celebrations of sexuality on the screen. Now I can watch those kinds of experiences on the screen with absolute comfort, but when I see just overt violence on the screen, I find myself reeling back, and not really enjoying that so much—not even accepting it.

I just used a simple example there, but the point I'm trying to make is that in my life I've learned to look at whatever makes me uncomfortable, then to move into more of the experience of that, because there's probably something there that I want to heal, or, at the very least, closely explore, to see whether it's serving me to be discomforted by that.

So when I say that life begins at the end of your comfort zone, I really mean that. On this side of our comfort zone is not real life, but kind of a slow death. I think people should be uncomfortable at least six times a day. And if you're not, *do something* that makes you uncomfortable. Give a speech, sing a song, dance a dance. Go to see a movie with lots of sexuality in it.

So, in the moment that I start feeling uncomfortable, I say: "Oh, there's that feeling of discomfort again. Yes, yes, bring it on." I'm actually comfortable with my discomfort—if that can make any sense.

Do you understand the Divine Dichotomy? I find comfort in my discomfort, that initial moment of—"Oh, I don't have"—"Not for me." The numbers have gotten larger. I was asked to make a contribution a while ago to a very important cause, and I wrote a thought down: "Well, you know—Practice what you preach." So, I wrote a check for ten thousand dollars to this particular cause. Okay. And I'm writing the check, and I'm going, "Even for me, this is not a small number . . . " I start breathing heavy, you know. Start breathing heavy. Wrote the check out, actually put it in the envelope. Should I really mail this? But that feeling of discomfort, that "Uh, uh, I'm not really sure, I'm not really sure," means I'm absolutely sure. It means that the highest part of myself is speaking to me—in a way that vibrates throughout every cell in my body, that I used to call discomfort, and that I now call a signal from the divine. Move into that, not away from it.

Every time I have denied myself the experience of my own greatness, it's because I've moved away from, rather than into, my discomfort—and locked myself out from my place of joy. Not once in a while, not now and then. *Every single time.*

Now, there are those among you that say, "But what of caution?" To which I say, "Throw caution to the wind. What can you lose but everything?" And until you're willing to lose it all, you cannot have it all. Because you think it's about holding on to what it is you now have. And that to which you hold on, will slip through your fingers. Yet that which you let go will come back to you sevenfold. Because your holding on to something dearly, for dear life, is the grandest announcement that you think that you are separate from it and everyone else.

See, I'm over here, and you're over there. And I've got this stuff, and I've got to hold on to it.

But your letting *go* is the grandest announcement that you're clear that there's no place where you end and I begin. Therefore, in a very real sense, when I let go of it to you, I give it back to myself.

Here are three words to always remember. Have these words tattooed on your left wrist: *Be the source.*

Be the source of that which you would choose for another. Come from that place of: I am the source.

If you want more magic in your life, bring more magic into the room with you. If you want more love in your life, bring more love into the room with you. If you want more joy in your life, bring more joy into the room with you.

Be the source, in the lives of others, of that which you would have in your own life.

If you want more money in your life, bring more money into the life of another. Whatever it is you want more of . . . if you want more compassion in your life . . . If you want more wisdom in your life, be the source of wisdom in the life of another. If you want more patience, more understanding, more kindness, more sex . . . the point is, it works. It *works*. It's delicious.

And through this process and the process of beingness, the process of being who you really are, you will bring yourself the experience of right livelihood virtually overnight. And the world will shower upon you all the rewards for which you reached in vain for so many years.

So, allow your doingness to spring from your place of beingness. Be happy, be abundant, be wise, be creative, be understanding, be a leader, be who you really are, in every moment of your life. Come from that place, and let your doingness spring from that place. And you'll not only find right livelihood, you will have created for yourself a life, rather than a living.

In closing

I do not consider myself a superficial person. I see the problems of scarcity, lack, and poverty that plague the world. I understand that for the largest portion of the Earth's inhabitants the word abundance, as most people now use it, has little meaning. More meaningful, to them, is the word *survival.*

I am also clear that this does not have to be. None of us should have to worry about day-to-day survival. That should be guaranteed, as should the basic human dignity of sufficient food, clothing, and shelter for all. Why we, as humans, do not share more freely of all that we have (a tiny percentage of the world's people holds a massive percentage of the world's wealth and resources), is no mystery. Most people believe in "lack." That is, they believe—even those with a great deal (perhaps, *especially* those with a great deal) believe—that there is "not enough to go around." Or, put another way, if *everyone on the planet* had a fair share, then those of us who have a *disproportionate* share would not have "enough."

This leads to a not unimportant question. When is "enough" enough?

For people whose chief reward in life, whose highest satisfaction and grandest experience, is derived from their quality of being, *whatever they now have* is enough. That is the lesson that some spiritual masters who give up everything and live lives of renunciation are seeking to teach. They do not seek to demonstrsate that renunciation is necessary to achieve true happiness. They seek merely to show that material possessions are *not* necessary.

Yet when a high state of beingness is turned into doingness in the physical world, one has achieved Right Livelihood, and struggle disappears from our lives, to be replaced by true abundance. After I read this in the *Conversations with God* books, I yearned to know, in a practical sense, how to do this. I earnestly wanted to know how to transform my activity in the work-a-day world into a sacred expression of Who I Really Am.

The result was an inspiration that produced a small book, called *Bringers of the Light*, which those who have read it have told me has brought understanding, at last, to this mystery of life. This little book is available from ReCreation, the non-profit foundation that Nancy and I formed a few years ago to help handle all the incoming energy (now almost 300 letters a week from all over the world) that has resulted from the publication of *Conversations with God*, and to spread its message.

If you are looking for a more interactive experience, each year the foundation presents three five-day intensives, "Recreating Your Self." Based on the messages in *CWG*, they are designed especially for those who are looking closely at the lives they are currently experiencing, and seeking ways that they can bring about real change.

For more information on these retreats, write:

CWG Recreating Your Self Retreats
ReCreation Foundation
PMB #1150
1257 Siskiyou Blvd.
Ashland, OR 97520

In addition, many questions on abundance—and, for that matter, all of the issues covered in the *Conversations with God* material—are addressed in the regular newsletter of the foundation. (We named the foundation ReCreation because of the message of CWG that the purpose of life is to recreate yourself anew in the next grandest version of the greatest vision ever you held about Who You Are.) The newsletter contains questions from readers everywhere on how to do just that. I answer each letter personally.

If you would like to "stay connected" with the energy of *CWG*, you may obtain a 12-issue subscription to the letter by sending $35 ($45 for addresses outside the U.S.) to the foundation.

Finally, Hampton Roads Publishing Company has produced a wonderful collection of the best of these queries and responses over the past five years, entitled *Questions and Answers on Conversations with God.* It and the *CWG Guidebook* (also from Hampton Roads) are two of the most helpful books ever produced for those who truly seek to understand the *CWG* material more fully, and to find practical ways to apply it in their everyday lives.

By these and other means, I hope that we can all learn more about abundance, what it really is, and how to experience it. I hope that we'll all remember how to share freely of everything that we have, and are. I know that some of us do. But once upon a time, all of us did. We knew how to live without expectation, without fear, without neediness, and without having to have power over someone, or to be somehow better than another. If we can get back to that place, we can heal our lives, and heal the world.

Blessèd be.